Don't Just Speak It, Write It

Don't Just Speak It, Write It

How Every Pastor Can
Become a Published Author

Don Newman

Xulon Press

Xulon Press
2301 Lucien Way #415
Maitland, FL 32751
407.339.4217
www.xulonpress.com

Printed in the United States of America.

ISBN-13: 978-1-54563-097-6

CONTENTS

ENDORSEMENTS

It is a pleasure to challenge every Christian leader to consider writing a book for the benefit of Kingdom expansion. Don Newman is one who can show you the way. In his book, *Don't Just Speak It, Write It: How Every Pastor Can Become A Published Author*, Newman helps the novice writer learn how to carve out the time and take the journey into the realm of a published Christian author. Writing a book is hard and not for everyone, but if you think it might be for you then know there are several spiritually beneficial reasons to go this route. You never know what plans God might have for the message he's given you. Within these pages you will discover why you should write, what writing a book can do for your ministry, mistakes to avoid in writing, and how to get started.

Tom Cheyney,
Founder & Directional Leader
Renovate National Church Revitalization Conference
Executive Editor, The Church Revitalizer Magazine
Multi-Book Author

"I tell leaders '*If God speaks to you... you might want to write it down!*' Most leaders I know talk about writing a book, but never take the steps necessary to do so. Don has helped so many take the steps necessary to fulfill that vision. He did it with me and he can do it for you. Every aspiring writer should read this and allow Don to help!"

Shawn Lovejoy

Founder & CEO of CourageToLead.com

Author

FOREWORD

When I was 22 years-old, I felt called to write a book.
I was a graduate student at Trinity International University when I heard God say in that still small voice, "Mark, I want you to be a voice to your generation." My spirit immediately discerned that as a call from God to write—despite the fact that I didn't do much writing or even reading, and I had just taken a graduate assessment test that revealed a low aptitude for writing. I was about to become exhibit A that God doesn't call the qualified; He qualifies the called.

It started by taking my sermons and turning them into evotionals (a fun name I coined for email devotionals) during the week. I dubbed those emails a "double dose"—you could hear my latest sermon first, and then if you liked it you could read it a few days later. I started blogging regularly and seizing any opportunity I could to hone my craft. For thirteen years, I was sharpening my ability to wield words on paper as well as the pulpit, but still all I had to show for it was a handful of half-finished manuscripts.

That's when I stumbled upon Ecclesiastes 11:4: "Farmers who wait for perfect weather will never plant" (NLT). A supernatural switch flipped in my spirit, and armed with that divine determination I self-imposed a hard deadline that I would not turn 35 years old without a book to show for it.

That gave me a total of 40 days. I finished my first manuscript, and self-published I.D.: True You. A year later, I wrote In a Pit with a Lion on a Snowy Day, and since then, I've published 15 more books. I've been fortunate enough to have some of those titles hit bestseller lists, including the New York Times bestseller list. Some have sold more copies than I would have had a category for when I first felt called to write. And I give God all the credit because He's the one who puts the right book in the right hands at the right time. My job? To write for an audience of one!

I can honestly say that being obedient to the calling to write those books changed the footprint of my ministry. It's allowed me to reach millions of people I would never have reached from my pulpit in Washington, D.C.

If there's a mantra of mobilization to Don't Just Speak It, Write It, that's it: the hours spent learning and laboring over one-on-one ministry, counseling your congregation, and writing sermons will send out holy ripples in your immediate vicinity. Amass that knowledge into a book, and those ripples push out further. They build in mass and momentum until they reach distant shores like waves from an anointed tsunami.

Need more proof? I've got one question... Have you heard Paul preaching lately? Listened to his latest sermon?

No, but I bet you've read a few of his epistles!

Don Newman has combined the pastoral passion he built during decades in ministry with the knowledge he gained while publishing two of his own books, and as an acquisitions director for a Christian publishing company. He's seen firsthand what the right book in the right hands at the right time can do. *Don't Just Speak It, Write It* is the culmination of all the wisdom that can be found at the crossroads of those two vocations. It's a call-to-arms for Christian leaders to use every megaphone possible to spread the good news, including books.

Rest assured, if you're holding this copy of Don't Just Speak It, there's a good chance it's in the right hands and the right time.

Mark Batterson
Lead Pastor National Community Church
New York Times Best Selling Author

INTRODUCTION

I heard a story a few years back about two pastors who took England by storm in the middle of the nineteenth century. According to the story, both of these pastors experienced great success as their congregations exploded and gained recognition for being successful growing churches. Both of these men were held in high regard for their work and their stance for Christ. One of them was Charles Haddon Spurgeon, known by many as the prince of preachers. The other was forgotten and to this day no one actually knows his name. The difference between the two is that one of them wrote books, and one of them did not. While I have never been able to actually prove the validity of this story, the point is well taken. A pastor who chooses to write and publish what God has given him has much more opportunity to influence others beyond his own congregation and generation.

Over the years, I have helped hundreds of pastors, evangelists, and church leaders write books that began as only a dream. In all that time, I have found no one is equipped and prepared to become an author like a pastor. Although it can take hours of convincing, once they see how prepared they really are, their desire to make a difference through writing grows exponentially. No one author is like any other, just as no one pastor is like any other. I've found while coaching pastors on how to write books that become beloved, dog-eared, highlighted tomes, they all have the same obstacles to overcome. The key is helping them see what they have and how they could move it into a written form that communicates the treasure God has given them.

The motivation for writing this book was not just to add another book to the growing list of books I have authored. I wrote this book with the intention that it would be used to inspire and enlist hundreds of pastors to write and publish books that leave a lasting legacy in print.

My two favorite questions to ask pastors when they are pondering whether or not they should commit to the process of writing a book are this: first, I ask them "What would the world be like today if men like Charles Spurgeon, John Wesley, C. S. Lewis, and Billy Graham never took the time to write? How would our world be?"

The second question I ask is, "If you could write a book that would be personally handed to your great-great-grandchildren, what would that book be about and why?" It's amazing what happens when a ministry leader realizes the scope of impact they can have through writing.

As you read this book, I pray you will allow yourself the chance to dream and discover how your big idea might just be the next best-selling book. Maybe your last sermon series is destined to become your next book. Who could be waiting for you to begin the journey of writing and sharing what God has showed you? If you would like more information on how you could become a published author, visit PastorEvent.com.

- CHAPTER 1 -

WHY SHOULD YOU WRITE A BOOK?

You've been thinking and praying about writing a book for months, maybe even years. No matter what you do, it simply never goes away; it continues to resurface time and time again. Sometimes it's just a passing thought and other times it's a *passionate* idea you cannot ignore. Someone may have even said to you, "That teaching is amazing, have you ever thought about writing a book?" Maybe you've heard someone say, "You really should put your story in a book." Maybe God has spoken to your heart and while you don't know *how*, you do know you *should* write a book. I have heard these accounts and many others as I have worked with hundreds of pastors and Christian leaders to get their first book published. Time and time again, leaders tell me the reasons they feel called to write a book and I can sense the eternal impact that each book might be destined to create. When you begin to think you are helping someone create a spiritual book that will ultimately outlive them, plus change lives they may never personally encounter, it is amazing!

What does a book *actually* do? A book takes a story or message that is within someone's mind or soul and moves it into print where others can read it and benefit from it. What does a Christian book do? A Christian book does the same thing, but it adds to the message or story the gifts and anointing of the one who writes it. Just look at your own favorite Christian books that are dog-eared and highlighted and ask yourself, "How did this book influence me? What gift, insight, or anointing touched my own life and ministry as I read through it?" Maybe it was just one statement on page ninety-four, but your life was never the same after reading it, even if you didn't notice it at first.

If you're already sharing your message through preaching or just one-on-one evangelism, you should take it a step further and move it into a book. A book, unlike a spoken message, leaves a legacy in print for the future and has the ability to impact people you may never get the chance to impact. More specifically, a book instructs, inspires, and affects readers so God can powerfully change their lives. For example, Charles Spurgeon, John Maxwell, and Max Lucado have impacted millions of lives by publishing books from their sermons and their ideas. Can you imagine how different the Christian world would be without the writings of Charles Spurgeon, D. L. Moody, or Andrew Murray? We were not alive when they spoke, but they are impacting generations of believers over and over again. They were able to move their messages into the printed form so they live on even after having gone to be with the Lord. They did it and so can you!

Christian books are conceived when you connect with God and a message or story forms within your heart or mind. The message takes form as your own heart is touched, but growth begins as you see it meeting a need or answering a question in the heart of someone else.

Great books come out of a combination of a message received and a need perceived.

As simple as it sounds, a Christian book is the answer given to someone to meet a need or desire within someone else. I love how Mark Batterson puts it:

> I have a handful of prayers that I pray all the time... One is that God will put my books into the right hands at the right times. I've prayed this prayer thousands of times, and God has answered it in dramatic fashion countless times. The right book in the right hands at the right time can save a

marriage, avert a mistake, demand a decision, plant a seed, conceive a dream, solve a problem, and prompt a prayer. That is why I write. And that's why, for me, a book sold is not a book sold; a book sold is a prayer answered. I don't know the name and situation of every reader, but God does, and that's all that matters.

— Mark Batterson, *Draw the Circle:*
The 40 Day Prayer Challenge

I love hearing stories of how God has used a book to change someone's life. I truly believe a book can change ten thousand lives or one life that changes ten thousand lives. I have heard great men and women of God share how a book changed their life or ministry. Usually that is when everyone, including me, desires that same type of change; we buy the book for ourselves and we dig into it with a full desire to receive our own life-changing moment.

One of my favorite stories from a writer I know very well comes from Dr. Larry Keefauver, the best-selling author of sixty books.

I was speaking to a group of international educators from North and South America, Europe, and Asia. Many of them used my college-level, online and DVD courses in their Bible schools and college curricula on marriage, family, and parenting. While I was speaking, a group of about twenty people in the back were making quite a bit of noise that was distracting as they were talking with each other. Irritated, but pushed for time, I continue to speak louder and more emphatically. As my volume increased, so did theirs.

My twenty-minute speaking limit came. I closed my talk, and walked away from the podium as the entire conference was dismissed for a morning coffee break. Suddenly, the noisy group from the back rushed up to me led by their excited ringleader. "I am the interpreter for this group," he explained. "Sorry for my noise but everyone in our group from the Ukraine was so thrilled when you, Dr. Larry, were introduced before your talk. All of them recognized you from your course and book on marriage which they have been studying."

I know I looked puzzled. Before I could speak, the animated, Russian interpreter went on, "You see, a few months ago our Bible school started your new course on Christian marriage with your textbook that had just arrived in Russian, *Lord I Wish My Husband Would Pray with Me: Tearing Down the Walls in Marriage.* Only one copy arrived, so we tore the book apart chapter by chapter and each couple got one chapter, read it, and then passed it on to another couple in the class. Already, over a dozen couples have been reading your book, which is blessing them and helping their marriages heal and grow. Thank you."

I was speechless. I had not been aware that my book, already translated in Spanish, Mandarin, and Portuguese, was now in Russian. God works in mysterious ways through books touching people even in faraway places. I am so grateful I had been obedient to write. I have learned that someone, somewhere in the world, is waiting on the other side of a writer's obedience to "write the book" to meet needs, answer questions, and change lives through books that God writes through us and sends to others with His grace, mercy, and love.

When you begin to understand your book, the one you are supposed to write, could have a similar impact, it changes how important it is to write it. I will never direct anyone to write for profit or gain alone. The world would be without books like *Pilgrims Progress* or other great classics if those authors had only decided to write if they could have material gain. In fact, some of the greatest classics came not as a gain, but as a potential loss. When I think of men like Dietrich Bonhoeffer, who was willing to pay the ultimate price not only through his ministry but also through his writing, I see the real reason and motivation why most Christian authors write and publish their books. They want to make an impact in the world for God! The book you are called to write probably will not cost you your life, but it will cost you. It will cost you time, effort, and the willingness to make it happen so it can accomplish what it is born for. Yes, it will cost you, but it will also pay you back in ways you can never imagine. Even if it never sells a copy outside your own church or family, it will be worth it. One of my favorite sayings I received in prayer one day is, "If it has the ability to change one heart, then it has the ability to change hundreds of hearts."

If it has the ability to change one heart, then it has the ability to change hundreds of hearts.

Almost every pastor or Christian leader I have coached ultimately agrees that nothing has the impact a Christian book can have. Even if their future book is only read by their family and descendants, it's still well worth doing. If this is the case, why do so many fail to move the idea from the inspiration stage to a finished book? They struggle because of what I call the "roadblocks of writing." The road to becoming a published author can be both difficult and confusing, especially when the challenges or roadblocks are scattered along the route every mile or so. However, it all begins with simply getting started.

GETTING STARTED IS THE CHALLENGE

Publishing is easy, but writing a book is another story. It can be hard at times. Notice, I said *hard* and *not impossible*. Simply put, writing a book takes commitment, but if you will take that step, cross that line, and write the book God has called you to write, it will change your life and the lives of your congregation or the people to which you minister.

We need pastors and front-line thinkers to keep writing. Mark Batterson, pastor of National Community Church in Washington, DC stated:

> I honestly believe that most people have at least one book in them. The problem is that many people go to the grave with their book still in them. Why? Nine times out of ten, they never finish the book because they never start it. I think the first chapter is the hardest chapter. It's a downhill coast from there. You need to find a metaphor, find your voice.
>
> —Mark Batterson,
> *You Have a Book in You*

Will your book be a best seller? No one knows, but I can tell you this, it will be a no seller if you never write it.

WHAT BLOCKS MOST PASTORS FROM WRITING THEIR BOOKS?

While I've said starting a book is hard, do you know what's harder? It's making the first real decision to start. Yes, your first hurdle is making a decision to just do it—to actually get'er done. That's when the real battle begins. Everything in the natural and supernatural realms will team up against you getting started. At the end of this book, I have an appendix concentrating on getting started. Be sure to read it if you decide to obey God's call on you and come back to it when you need encouragement to keep moving forward.

Let me list for you the most common excuses for not leaving a legacy in print.

EXCUSE #1 — I DON'T HAVE THE TIME

I can have a powerful conversation with a pastor or leader where they clearly see the vision of the book and the impact it could have on others. They see it, but all too many times I hear the same thing, "I just don't have the

time to write it." Being a former pastor myself, and one
that was bi-vocational, I not only understand the com-
ment, but I also agree with it. The truth is no one really has
time for writing a book. Yes, there is the fantasy of living
at the beach and having days upon days to write great,
moving books, but that fantasy only exists for the retired
or the extreme wealthy. Yes, some fantasize if they could
be carefree then they could write, but the truth is when
most people become carefree they most often are dis-
tanced from the real world and the questions people ask
every single day. Unlike them, most pastors and Christian
leaders are knee-deep in the mud with everyone else.
Yes, the people who are best suited to write in light of the
real world and God are all very busy.

If pastors don't have time, especially if they are bi-vocational, then how can they write the book burning on
their heart or in their mind? Again, no one has the time,
so like everyone else you have to make the time. Getting
beyond this hindering excuse is simpler than you imagine.
It begins by making a commitment of time within your
week. As you block out your time, keep in mind there is
more than one way to write a book. I have a pastor friend
who dictates the core message of his sermon into his
phone in fifteen-minute segments each week and then
emails the audio files to a volunteer who transcribes for
him. In fact, this book was actually started by speaking
certain portions on my phone while I drove to work. I was

able to record voice memos and then send them to my editor who moved them into written form. Whether you write on a computer or dictate recordings that are transcribed, *just do it.* It can be as little as fifteen minutes in audio, or writing two hundred and fifty words, or completing two pages a day. You know the adage: *How do you eat an elephant? One bite at a time.*

One leader confessed to me that he couldn't do even fifteen minutes a day, but then admitted he had a two-hour block every Sunday in which he could write. Finally, he blocked the time on his calendar as an irrefutable appointment between him and the Lord to write as he was called. Yes, the first step is the hardest, but if you will make the commitment, you will start. Almost every time I coach someone through the "I don't have the time" issue, they always tell me something like this, "Man, I started writing in the morning. At first, I didn't know what to write, but then it came to me and I didn't want to stop. I wrote over five hundred words in less than an hour." It's amazing how the excuse of not having enough time goes away when someone learns there is actually a book within them. Writing a book is like running a race; you have to start it and then you will find you can do it. Start the race and then tell me that you do not have the time.

Running the race means you have to leave the blocks. Get started.

EXCUSE #2 — I DON'T FEEL MY STUFF IS WORTHY

Neither did the Apostle Paul, but look at the best seller his letters have been for almost two thousand years. While there is no doubt he was writing something completely different from any book written today, it is important to understand that he didn't know how worthy his writing would one day be while he was writing. Paul wrote because God wanted him to and it was his passion.

What should you do if you feel this way? First, you should understand that every great writer has struggled with these same feelings. No one writes a book they are absolutely sure will become everyone's most favorite book. Then why do people write, especially Christian authors? It's because they feel led to do so and because they have a passion about something they simply have to share.

Ask yourself these questions:

1. If I get to the end of my life and I never wrote this book, would I regret it?

12

2. If I knew there was one person in the world who would come to Christ or change their life for the better, would I definitely write this book?

If your answer to both of these questions is yes or even one answer is yes, then despite your fears, you should still write your book. In the end, you should ask yourself, "Is the book I dream of writing meant for my success or for the success of others?" If it is written with a passion, then it is written for others. Write about your passion and you will impact others! The Old Testament word for "passion" is zeal. The promise is that the zeal of the Lord will accomplish the very thing that's needed. God's desires are not impossible. Let Him light your fire and inspire your words. The Holy Spirit will give you the words you need.

In the New Testament, the word "passion" is used in Acts 1 to refer to the Lord's passion—His suffering and death. Now, in the secular world, passion is often rooted in ego or arrogance. In Christ, passion is rooted in being crucified to self and made alive through His power, mercy, and grace. When you die to your flesh, and that includes your excuses and weaknesses, His power and strength will empower and inspire you to move forward in obedience and faith. Many times, I want to say to a leader who is worried his book will not be a best seller. "Get over yourself and think about who needs to read what you have to write." Become the pen of a ready writer in the hand of Christ. Get yourself out of the way of what God wants to do through you with your book. Remember, someone is waiting for His message that can only come through you. Will you obey so they can receive from Christ? No one is worthy, but Christ in you, serving others through you, makes it worthwhile, essential, and necessary.

You may have a passion about a certain subject, but are afraid someone else has already written about it and done a better job than you could do. I have assured thousands of potential authors and I confidently declare to you:

Whether your book changes and impacts ten thousand people or just one person, it is worthy to be written.

Many years ago, a church leader and friend gave me a book titled, *Deeper Experiences of Famous Christians* by James Gilchrist Lawson. There are several stories in the book about famous Christians, like George Whitefield and D. L. Moody. There is one story about a man called Elder Jacob Knapp who lived during the 1800s.

When I ask people if they have ever heard of the author James Gilchrist Lawson, most say they have not. When I ask people if they have ever heard of Elder Jacob Knapp, almost all of them say they have not. I then tell them on page 199 of *Deeper Experiences of Famous Christians* there is a statement that changed my life forever. You see, this book was given to me when I was young and ignorant—a people pleaser who would do anything and everything my pastor told me to do in hopes of getting into the ministry. My desire to please my pastor caused problems in my family and with my wife. The story of Elder Jacob Knapp was about him being a people pleaser, dealing specifically with his trouble getting backing from his denomination to pursue his calling as an evangelist. Like me, he struggled as he tried to get man's approval over God's approval. Finally, in his distress, he called out to God during a fast and God asked him, "Have I not given you a field to labor in?"

When Knapp answered *yes,* God then told him, "Then go and labor in the field I have given you and don't worry about them." Knapp ended up leading thousands of people to Christ. God spoke to me through that one story from a book by an author no one has ever heard of and it changed my life from that point. I am so glad that James Gilchrist Lawson wrote that book and wrote the story of Elder Jacob Knapp. Today, I am no longer a man pleaser and God has done many wonderful things through my own life and ministry because of the change I experienced reading a book that never made it to the New York Times best-selling list.

I believe there are books meant to make the New York Times best-sellers' list and I believe there are books that make God's list of life-changing books. Sometimes, a book can be both a best seller and a life changer, but if I had to pick one, I choose life changing every time.

If God has given you a passion for something, then someone needs to hear it. It's up to you to write it so they can read it.

A book can change ten thousand lives, or it can change one life that changes ten thousand lives.

EXCUSE #3 — AREN'T THERE ALREADY BOOKS OUT THERE ABOUT THIS SAME SUBJECT?

This question begs the question, "Why should I write mine?" It's true, there are few subjects for which books have not already been written. However, I tell leaders that books are like snowflakes—no two are exactly the same. I ask them to think about their favorite book and if they have made highlights in it or in some other way marked certain pages or passages; most say yes. The reason people do this is because they have not read that particular point written in that particular way in any other book. It is fresh and new to them despite being a topic covered elsewhere. It is something that touches them in a specific moment in a specific way when they are most attuned to receiving it.

I had another book given to me that was called *Soul Keeping* by John Ortberg. It's an incredible book, and I highly recommend it for addressing the importance of taking care of one's inner or spiritual life. Throughout the book, the author talks about his unique relationship with Dallas Willard and how Dallas impacted his life. In one conversation, Ortberg asked Willard how he could keep himself spiritually strong amidst all the busyness and time constraints of ministry. Willard told the author he would need to ruthlessly eliminate hurry. When I read Dallas Willard's answer, I highlighted it and said to myself, "This is exactly what I needed to hear at this very moment in my life."

While I have read and reread this great book several times, the section that impacted me the most was the story of that conversation Ortberg had with Willard. That story will not be found in its entirety in any other book in the world. Likewise, even if your book is written on a subject that has been published over a hundred times this year, it will still contain stories, illustrations, and anecdotes not found in any other book in the world. Again, just look at the books on your shelf and look at what you highlighted. Sometimes you read the right book, but most times, you read the right page in the right book.

It is not the whole book that impacts the reader. It is that one statement that is found in that one book that was meant for that one reader.

All of us have a unique story someone else needs to read. Though another book may exist on the same subject, you need to realize someone may need your book solely because they will never read the other book. Your story can make a difference in someone's life or they may give your book to someone who can only receive the message by reading your book with *your* insight from your perspective.

To have a great book, you need to have someone who lives it or sees it, and then writes about it.

EXCUSE #4 — I WANT MY BOOK TO BE PERFECT

Someone once said perfectionism is the mother of procrastination and that is especially true in the world of writing. I have heard multiple excuses on countless occasions that relate back to issues with perfectionism. Some concern having the perfect knowledge, such as, "I have to wait until I *know* I can write the perfect book," or "I have to wait until I have my master's degree." Other excuses concern the perfect timing. My favorites are, "I have to wait until my church is successful" or "I can only write after I have had twenty-five years in the ministry." To this last one, I always point out the great books published while someone was in the process of building their church or ministry. I'm not saying you should publish a book on how to plant churches if you've never planted one, but **we learn best from people who are learning themselves**. I have seen people who have a great message fail to ever write a chapter simply because they can only move if it will be perfect. My response to perfectionism excuses is always, "There is no perfect book except the Bible." God uses *imperfect* books every day to impact others.

There is a big difference between an imperfect book that is read and a perfect book that has never been written.

If you wait to write when you think you have the perfect book or the perfect situation to become an author, you may miss the window of timing meant for your book. Don't let perfection give birth to procrastination.

WHY PASTORS MAKE GREAT AUTHORS

Pastors and those who minister are ready to become authors more than they realize. When you think about the preaching they are doing every week, you realize their first or subsequent book may already exist in a sermon or outline. Most pastors are studying and consciously preparing for sermons they feel are relevant to their congregation. They are already wrapping information around segments as they prepare for their sermons every week, which places them ahead of most authors who have to study and research their material before they can begin writing. A pastor also knows how to communicate ideas. A book is nothing more than a tool—a tool used to communicate. More than anything the pastor, when he is operating correctly, is in tune with his congregation and with God. Knowing what people are going through, and knowing where God is leading them, is the key. When a pastor understands the questions and concerns people are dealing with, he can marry those ideas with direction from God to deliver a message that resounds in the hearts of his congregation. The same is true with a book. The method a pastor uses to write his sermons can also be used to write his book.

Most pastors don't realize their last sermon may very well be their next book.

I love to help pastors and Christian leaders cross the bridge to become authors because I know the effects this can have on their life and ministry. When they see that some of their sermons or a sermon series can be expanded into a book, they begin to realize the many benefits they can bestow to their congregation and to others they may never meet.

Ask Yourself...

At the end of each chapter, I will ask you to answer questions in writing. Keep a dated notebook and journal. Write down your prayer requests about writing and publishing. Be sure to also write down the dreams, visions, insights, wisdom, and answers God gives you.

- *Am I committed to leaving a legacy in print?*
- *Am I ready to plan my weekly writing schedule?*
- *When will I start?*
- *To whom will I be accountable?*
- *When (the date) will I finish writing my first book?*
- *What is that book's working title?*
- *What is the source of the material—messages, speeches, computer files, journals, notebooks, dictation, etc.?*
- *What is my business plan for writing and publishing in regards to time line, budget, putting together*

a team to coach me and hold me accountable, setting goals and objectives, and praying daily through the whole plan?

- CHAPTER 2-

WHAT WRITING A BOOK WILL DO FOR YOUR MINISTRY

One of the reasons why I am so passionate about helping pastors and ministers write their own books is because I know how their writing will impact their ministries and their congregations. Over the years, I have worked with several pastors who wrote; I witnessed first-hand how their books impacted their ministries and the people to whom they ministered. I have found several things a book accomplishes for the pastor who writes one. Here are a few:

IT PRESERVES THEIR TEACHINGS FOR FUTURE GENERATIONS

I really believe pastors are to carry on a tradition that preserves our theological heritage from generation to generation. The Apostle Paul, the early church leaders,

23

the church fathers, and all the reformers were writers. They recorded their teachings and passed them on from generation to generation, a tradition modern-day pastors need to continue.

IT EXTENDS THEIR INFLUENCE BEYOND THE SUNDAY MESSAGE

Pastors need to write their sermons in book form as a way to influence and impact their congregation beyond Sunday and mid-week services. The books recording their sermons become reference books for their congregation members. Books that are read and digested provide the nuggets and insights that congregations need. Rick Warren came up with a program to focus on building the body of Christ in his own congregation. He then translated it into a book called *The Purpose Driven Life*. The book began as a teaching and went on to impact millions of hearts.

A pastor's book can move a message deeper into the hearts of his congregation. A. W. Tozer said he was not writing his books for the professional theologian, instead he wanted to stir the hearts of his own congregation to seek a deeper relationship with God.

Publishing a book is also a way to get the vision and heart of the ministry into each and every person who comes to church. The pastor's book reflects his vision and helps everyone involved to stay focused on that vision.

IT BECOMES A TOOL FOR THEIR CONGREGATION

The books a pastor publishes can also be used by their congregation to reach out to others beyond their church family. For example, consider a pastor who does a series of teachings on "How to Raise a Teenager" which he writes into a book. It is obvious to see how this impacts his own congregation, but suppose a member has a neighbor who is having trouble with his teenager. That church member might talk with his neighbor about how he used the pastor's book to help with his own teenager. He may then offer the book as a way of helping the neighbor with his teenager. Now, this neighbor might not join the church, but receiving the pastor's book can help him deal with an issue happening in his life right then and there. This is how a pastor can extend his message beyond his congregation and impact people elsewhere. A pastor never knows who his books might be passed on to in the future. His teaching can possibly reach, and impact, others far away from his own sphere of personal influence.

Books also live on to impact future generations, carrying important lessons forward. For example, I discovered I have several pastors in my family tree. One of them is Samuel Newman, my six times removed great-grandfather on my father's side who lived in South Carolina during the 1760s. Another relative is Charles Wesley Pope, who was a Baptist pastor in Tennessee back in the 1950s. I soon learned of his leadership in the body of Christ and at

Carson Newman College. As I continued to research him, I learned he had written a book titled, *Is Life Worth Living*, which is based on his sermons and teachings through the book of Ecclesiastes. This was born out of his years as a pastor and teacher at the college.

I was so excited when I was able to secure a copy of his book written so many years ago. He had published 200 copies or so and sold them for $2.50 a copy, but his book is priceless to me. It is a family treasure I will be passing to my children and my grandchildren. For that legacy alone, his writing it was worth it. My ancestor's book has inspired my family and thousands of people to whom I have told his story to again and again. Would he ever have dreamed when he was writing his book that I would be talking about it today?

Since then, I discovered another one of my great, great-uncles also wrote a Christian book while he was serving as a pastor. Both of my relatives' books proudly stand on my bookshelf at home. I also carry them with me to conferences to talk about the importance of writing a book. Words written then are still speaking to generations today.

Every pastor needs to consider the spiritual heritage his book could impart and the baton he could pass along to future generations. Somewhere in your future lineage, someone is going to want to read about what you have taken the time to write about. I tell people, "writing lasts!"

IT MAKES THE PASTOR A BETTER COMMUNICATOR

Nothing can improve a pastor's ability to communicate one of his core messages like writing and publishing a book. When a pastor forces his message through the discipline of writing, he is also forcing his mind to make his message crystal clear for those who will encounter it. I have personally found that every pastor who writes his core message into a book never needs sermon notes when he is sharing it.

Writing is to the pastor like a sharpener is to the pencil, both bring clarity and definition.

WRITING YOUR BOOK WILL INSPIRE THE CURRENT GENERATION

Just by sharing what you have gone through in writing your book will inspire others who are being challenged by God to write their own book. A pastor who steps across the line to write challenges others to step across that line as well. Even those who do not feel the call to write will be challenged to cross other lines in pursuing God's plan for their lives. It is amazing how many people you might inspire by stepping across that line. You might be surprised to hear that 70 percent of the people in your congregation have a desire to write a book. One-third of them are serious, one-third of them are struggling because they do not know what to do, and for one-third it is just a pipe dream.

THE CHURCH IS IN NEED

At every conference I attend, I hear churches are not growing and are in need. The speakers often talk about what is wrong and many of them offer solutions for how to bring about change. I often think, "I hope he is writing a book." This is not because I see the potential of book sales, but because I know that many leaders within the Church really need to hear what these speakers say. Just as we have drawn on the wisdom of those who have come before us, today's pastors need to communicate what they have to share about meeting the needs of the church today.

I attended a very special meeting with Dr. Bill Bright toward the end of his life. Dr. Bright will always be known as someone who was not going to let the fear of risk stop him from attempting great things for God. In that meeting held in his home, Dr. Bright said, "We can't become like Europe where all the church buildings are closing and it boils down to one or two mega churches in each state." He went on to cast his vision for raising up leaders who could jump in early and help plant local churches all over the place. I was moved by what Dr. Bright said, and I, along with my wife, became some of those young leaders answering the call to enlist and make a difference.

You never know who God will call through your book.

A group of five missionaries were killed while on the mission field attempting to bring the Gospel to a remote tribe in Ecuador. It was a tragic story that led to an amazing breakthrough for God in that region. The wife of one of the missionaries, Elisabeth Elliot, wrote *Through Gates of Splendor* to share the story of the incident and what God ultimately did through it. This book has inspired countless hundreds of people to become missionaries even though the book talks about men losing their lives. It was because of what God said through this wife who wrote her husband's story that many have felt and followed the call to go. Today's pastors need to be obedient to God's call as well. They need to shepherd and lead their flocks, communicate truth, and share that truth in a way that compels others to follow Christ.

A book is simply communicating something God has put on your heart.

With today's struggles, if there was a time for men and women of God to step up, it is now. The sad thing is I witness many leaders share their solutions for bringing about change, but most times their message never gets beyond their own congregations. Just as we have drawn on the wisdom of those who have come before us, like Martin Luther, E. M. Bounds, and Leonard Ravenhill, today's pastors need to communicate what they have to share in regards to meeting the needs of the church today. Each of these great men wrote and communicated their message because there was a need in the church of their day. They communicated to their generation and they wanted God to be able to use it. They wrote something years ago and it still inspires people today because it lived on in written form.

THE CHAIN OF BOOK SALES

What do you do when you read a great book, see a great movie, or go to a great restaurant? You tell everyone you know about it. Peter Lord wrote what I consider to be the best book on hearing God's voice called, *Hearing God*. Someone gave me a copy of it, said it was a great book, and I read it. My wife and I both read it and decided it would be a great tool to use in the home group we were leading for college students. Each of us got a copy of the book to actively learn how to hear God's voice. Out of the forty people we took through that book, two of them went into ministry. Years later, I ran into one of those young men and he asked me the name of the book we had all gone through together years ago. I gave him my copy and he shared it with someone else who took a bunch of young people through it like we had done. Then, someone in that group did the same thing with another group in another church. When I followed the chain of sales of that book from my word of mouth, three hundred people had purchased it—all because someone gave me a copy and I passed it on. You never know who will be a future recipient of your book, but this brings to light the real secret behind all book sales. Books ultimately sell because someone reads it and shares something about it that leads someone else to read it as well.

The best person to sell your book is the last person who read your book.

THE FIRST PERSON YOUR BOOK WILL IMPACT IS YOU

By writing a book, a pastor not only becomes a better communicator and spiritual leader, he also changes through the writing process. Writing forces you to think clearly and crystalizes your thoughts. By forcing you to be precise and exact, your own mind and spirit have to push through the words you are choosing to write. The whole process of writing plants that material in you like a seed that you study and meditate on. As your message passes through you into your writing, it becomes a part of you. You literally breathe it out and communicate it more concisely then you would have if you had not written it.

You want to be able to do this with your message so you can perfect your "elevator pitch." You need to have your vision boiled down to a concise explanation you're able to share in an elevator ride. This means you can speak about your book's theme without needing notes; you can just share it because it is so much a part of you. Every time you speak on your subject after you have written it in a book, it will come out with deeper meaning, clarity, and precision because it has changed you. It's not just information—it has become an impartation.

The discipline of writing and rewriting is an invaluable formative process. Ideas tend to get clearer as the fog lifts, becoming bright and crisp. As a pastor learns to write consistently, he comes into a rhythm of life that is very impressive in what it does for him, both spiritually and intellectually. It is going to deepen the scriptures within you. Luther said it's the act of writing and rewriting the scriptures again and again that changes the author first.

Michael Waltrip is a NASCAR driver. He won a race at the Daytona Beach Speedway, but Dale Earnhardt Sr. died in a crash that happened right behind him. My son and I were at that race, sitting in the stands on the Super Stretch. Michael went through incredible guilt and turmoil during that time in his life, which affected his marriage and his spiritual life. Going through that very dark time moved him to write a book about it called, *In the Blink of an Eye: Dale, Daytona and the Day that Changed Everything*. It is about what he went through and how God walked him through the aftermath of that terrible day. He said, "I don't know if anybody is going to read it, but writing that book healed me!" The first person your book is going to minister to is *you*, but it won't stop there. The impact of it will touch others.

YOUR BOOK WILL OPEN DOORS

Another way your book will impact your life is by opening doors to you and to your ministry. Your book is the greatest business card you will ever have. Over the years, I have met pastors who became connected to another pastor or ministry simply because their book was shared. One of the greatest ideas I have seen on gaining speaking engagements came from a friend of mine. He offers to come and speak without requesting an honorarium or even a love offering. The only thing he requests is to be able to have a book table in the foyer. He preaches for free and sells his book for any gift donation. He often finds that his books bring more than any offering would, and it connects him to more people in the body of Christ.

Your book will not only open doors for you, it will communicate your message at a deeper level than you can in a 45-minute message. One of the most overlooked benefits of writing a book is the time it will ultimately save you. If your book is on prayer and someone asks to talk to you about prayer on the way out of the church, you can give them a copy of your book, ask them to read it, and then offer to meet with them at another time to discuss it. If they are serious about getting help, you will hear back from them after they have read your book.

One of the things I do at conferences is to offer a thirty-minute coaching session with pastors who believe they are called to write a book. I love doing this by the way; it's really become my ministry to ministers. I ask participants a series of questions and when we get done, they are on their way to writing their book. One pastor I did this with went away from that coaching session and met with one of our ghostwriters. He then went on to publish his very first book. A year later, I was asked to attend another conference and do a couple of workshops on writing. I told them I could do two of the workshops, but would not be able to do the last one. I recommended the pastor I had worked with, who had written his book a year earlier. I gave them his book and they said it was just what they were looking for. We set up a book signing at the conference and he did a breakout session. Then, he began to receive invitations to do more sessions. He has had numerous speaking engagements since then; it has grown his ministry and opened up doors all over the world. He just finished his second book. It would not have happened if he had not committed to and written that first book.

A pastor once said to me, "If you're not growing, you're dying." That's true for churches, businesses, and people. Keep your journal, a notebook, or your phone dictation app with you. Record every idea, thought, and truth you have for your book(s) as you listen to and observe everything around you. Even as you sleep, God will wake you to record dreams and revelations that He gives you in the night.

HERE'S YOUR CHECKLIST FOR MOVING FORWARD...
- Making a commitment to write and publish to God, to an accountability partner or group, and to yourself!
- Write the commitment down in a journal and date it.
- Keep God ideas for books in the journal.
- Develop a writing and publishing plan with dates you expect to reach for your goals and objectives. Some Christian leaders, pastors, and speakers or teachers make plans to write one book a year since they have accumulated more than enough material during that time.

- Read the appendix at the end of this book, *How to Get Started Writing Your Book.*
- Register at my website: CoachDonNewman.com. I will be sharing things on my site to help and encourage those who want to write a book.
- Write a prayer you will pray daily to keep writing and publishing your books before God.

Ask Yourself...

- *How can my book impact my ministry and/or congregation?*
- *What sermon series do I need to consider for my first or next book?*
- *What books have changed my life and ministry, and what can I learn from them?*
- *Who needs to read the book I am called to write?*
- *How do I see my future book impacting the Church and/or community?*
- *What would I like my future descendants to know about me and from me?*

- CHAPTER 3-

HOW DO YOU WRITE A GREAT CHRISTIAN BOOK?

There are some great keys everyone should follow when they are looking to write a great Christian book. Before I even get into all of the specifics of what, who, and how, it is important to establish some foundational principles. A great Christian book does not just come from a great Christian mind; it comes from a genuine Christian experience. When people ask me, *what drives Christian book sales*, it's not what most would expect—a desire to sell coupled with a demand to buy. It's more than that. Christian book sales are driven from a desire to tell, not just sell, that is coupled with a demand for impartation. It's what I like to call, "I want what you have, not just what you are selling."

There is nothing quite as important for an author then having his or her own genuine spiritual experience to draw from when writing a Christian book. In other words, the greatest thing any Christian author needs before they even think about writing a book is their own experience with God, through Jesus Christ. While this book will teach you how you move your experience into written form, whether it's nonfiction or fiction, it all must come from your own beautiful experience with the Son of God. From that relationship comes the inspiration, ideas, and words you will use to create something that ultimately leads others to be inspired, enriched, and immersed in their own walk with Jesus.

Writing a Christian book begins and ends with prayer.

Now that we have established where all great Christian books get their power and influence, what are the keys to how you write a Christian book? Two important elements to decide are "what" and "who."

WHAT ARE YOU GOING TO WRITE ABOUT?
Your subject should be something you are passionate about, something you are an expert in, or both. Being an expert simply means you know more than the guy next to you because you have a passion about it and have researched or lived it. Write about something that moves

you or stirs you up. When you think about some of the great Christian writers of our time, you can discover what they are passionate about by reading what they have written. Ask yourself the following questions:

1. What am I so passionate about that I am willing to take the time to spend writing it for others to read?
2. What I am so passionate about that it's easy to talk about, in fact I talk about it quite often?

WHO ARE YOU WRITING THE BOOK FOR?

Two of the highest selling self-published books are *The Shack* and *The Christmas Box*. Not everyone knows that both of those books were written specifically for the authors' children. *The Christmas Box*, by Richard Paul Evans, was written specifically as an expression of love for his two young daughters, Jenna and Allyson. Evans didn't have a real plan to ever publish or market the book for others to buy. It was the author's hope that one day, as his daughters read the book, they would realize how much he loved them as their father. The author had the book produced and only printed twenty copies to give to family and friends as a Christmas gift. As one person read the book and shared it with someone else, a growing demand appeared. That demand led to a book deal with Simon & Schuster for a very large amount. Today, *The Christmas Box* has sold well over eight million copies and was turned into an award-winning television movie in 1995, which starred Maureen O'Hara and Richard Thomas. To the author, his audience was two little girls whom he wanted to know exactly how much he loved them. He was passionate about the idea of creating a story that communicated the love of a father.

The Shack was also created by the author for his children. William Paul Young had no intention of becoming a published author. He was trying to write a story for his six children that communicated his own story of how God showed up and healed his heart. Once he had written and completed the book, he made fifteen copies at Office Depot and the rest was history. *The Shack* has gone on to break many records for a self-published book.

The keys to both of these best-selling books are the same we see in other successful authors. Evans and Young knew who they were writing to and why they were writing. Neither were pastors, nor were their books written specifically for Christians, but the same truth applies to many well-known Christian books written by Christian pastors or leaders. Whether it was Charles Spurgeon, A. W. Tozer, or Rick Warren, you can see their successful books came out of a message that was probably intended or originally directed to their own congregations. Their messages became books directed toward someone or some group. They were intended for a specific audience.

The misunderstanding a lot of people have about book writing is that if you write specifically for your children or your own congregation, no one else will read it. That is absolutely false. A pastor I know wrote a book specifically for men; surprisingly lots of women started reading it as well. That is because it is focused and on point. You need to write for a specific audience.

A book that is written for everyone is really written for no one.

WHAT MAKES A BOOK A PAGE-TURNER?

A *great* book has impact because it accomplishes three results. It either heals a hurt, meets a felt need, or answers questions. For example, imagine I am at a conference and I approach one of the pastors an hour and a half before he speaks and ask, "What are you going to speak on?" He'll tell me it's evangelism and how to plan for doing so in the upcoming year. Then imagine I inform him that 75 percent of the pastors he is going to speak to have been in ministry fifteen years or more, are fifty years or older, and are asking themselves, "Am I getting too old for this? Do I need to prepare to pass this responsibility on to someone else?" The pastor will probably adjust his message a little to better suit the audience.

While he will most likely continue to teach on evangelism and how you create a plan for it, he will most likely add a few points to address their concerns. I could imagine him saying something like, "If some of you are asking yourself if you are too old to start a new evangelism program, I just want to remind you of John Wesley who traveled in ministry by horseback or by foot well into his eighties."

The same focus on your audience is necessary when writing a book. Instead of just writing about a bunch of random points or principles, decide the questions you are going to answer for the specific group of people for whom you are writing your book.

I went to a self-publishing conference where the keynote speaker made an amazing point about how to write a successful book. He was passionate about skydiving, so he took lessons, joined a club, and thought about the stuff he wanted to learn about. Then he listened to the questions people were asking and the stories they were telling. He summarized the questions and the things people wanted to know, turned around, and wrote a book answering those questions. Then, he went back to the same people and sold them the book. He said to himself, "This is easy. Just write what you are passionate about and combine it with the things others would want to know about that subject. You will have a best seller!"

Ask Yourself...

- *What experiences have I had with God and/or on my journey of faith that I could be sharing?*
- *What message or teaching do I feel called to share with other Christians (or non-Christians)?*
- *Who exactly is my main audience? While many may read my book, who is the primary group I wish to impact?*
- *What need(s) am I meeting for my audience?*
- *What knowledge do I have on the subject that would be valuable to share?*

- CHAPTER 4 -

MISTAKES TO AVOID WHEN WRITING AND PUBLISHING YOUR BOOK

Over the many years I have coached authors, I am almost always asked questions on what someone should do to become a successful author. While it is important to know how to write a successful book, it is equally important to know what you want to avoid.

#1 – FAILING TO WRITE THE FIRST BOOK

I have often found myself thinking, "How many great books are buried in the graveyards of this country?" On more than one occasion, I have had to help family members publish the unfinished book of their lost loved one. Many times, these family members only have the notes or journals of the person, and they try to fulfill the original publishing dream as a way to pay tribute to their loved one. As I speak to these survivors, I often hear them say how the person they lost was always talking about writing a book one day. These encounters encourage me to say, "Never ever take your book to the grave where it can never help anyone."

I would rather deal with the disappointment of a book not selling than the regret that I never wrote it.

#2 – ATTEMPTING TO WRITE EVERYTHING IN ONE BOOK

I told one pastor who wanted to write a book that it was really five or six books. My exact words were, "If you put all that in one book, then you are writing an encyclopedia and no one is going to read it." If it's your first book, start by writing on the subject of your "home run" sermon series or your vision. An average book is about forty thousand words or just under two hundred pages. A pastor I know has taken each of his sermon series at a time, written it in book form, and offered it in the church bookstore. He keeps his books to sixty pages each, which is about twelve thousand words. The advantage of a short book is that a person can read it in one sitting.

#3 – TRYING TO WRITE THE PERFECT BOOK

I always tell new authors, "Don't get stuck in perfect land." Almost every pastor I work with who writes a book later sees something in their finished book they wish they could change. It just comes with the territory and things change over time. Something you see today, you will see a little differently in the future. I actually worked with one pastor who kept editing and changing his book over and over again, delaying its publication for years. I told him that the people who needed his book might have moved on or even died by the time he finished it. I can remember him saying, "But I want it to be the best it can be." I couldn't agree more, but I had to remind him of these two truths.

There is a big difference between an imperfect book that is read and the perfect book that was never written.

First, a book that touches someone's life in a positive way usually impacts the reader through a few key statements. Think about the books that have impacted your own life. When you look through them after reading them, do you find places you have dog-eared or highlighted? Those are the key places that impacted your life. I like to call those the "stars" or "lead actors" of the production. Everything else is the supporting cast. Those parts of the book are just as important, but they are not like the places you highlight and underline. That means you should work your book to a point and then release it to make the impact it's destined to make. Yes, get editing and proofreading, but stop when it's done and don't go back trying to make it better.

Second, it's important to know that you will never write a perfect book. I like to point out the fact that the works of some of today's famous authors have grammatical errors or misspelled words in them. It's amazing that even with the best editors there is still the opportunity to miss something. The crazy thing is that even with a misspelled word, these books still ended up published. As long as the book is meeting a felt need, healing a hurt, or answering a question, its imperfections will be overlooked. In the end, there is only one perfect book—the Bible.

#4 – NOT GETTING CONSTRUCTIVE FEEDBACK ON YOUR BOOK BEFORE PUBLISHING

Some authors are afraid of feedback, but I tell them I would rather find out what the people I trust like and don't like before the book is in print. Ask friends and family to read your manuscript and offer real, constructive feedback. Send it to those who are praying for you and ask them to read it with the homework assignment of telling you what would specifically make the book better. Ask them what is clear and what is confusing. See if they can summarize for you the main message of the book. Do the same when you get the draft cover of your book.

Likewise, doing a study guide to go with your book is a great idea, but make sure you have used it in a small group setting before you publish it so you can get genuine feedback from the group and see what works and what doesn't.

#5 – NOT HAVING YOUR BOOK PROPERLY EDITED

Editing is an important step in producing a book, and one that should not be skipped. Editing is what makes a good book great. As a writer, you are too close to your work and too emotionally connected to look at it objectively. You can't see it with the clarity and understanding a book editor uses.

An editor's job is not to change your message, your voice, or your tone, as some writers fear. Rather, an editor works to make sure what you are intending to communicate comes through clearly and concisely. Even bestselling authors submit their books to the editing process. It is key to having quality writing and a professional product. Review the appendix to learn more about the different types of editing you can explore.

Be sure to choose a professional editor. You are certain to have friends, coworkers, English teachers, and others in your circle who say they'll edit your book for free. These people are sure to be of benefit because they will catch some errors and give you the feedback I suggested you get in #4. Keep in mind, however, you get what you pay for. Professional editors are trained and experienced in developing a book to make it more marketable. It's a bit like getting your car fixed. Your handy neighbor might be perfect for changing the oil, but for that broken transmission, you are going to take the car to a certified mechanic.

#6 – NOT HAVING A PLAN TO MARKET AND SELL YOUR BOOK

Your marketing plan is simply a plan to create a desire for your book. For example, my mother is a great cook. When we were growing up, we would look forward to her amazing Sunday afternoon meals. She would start making things on Friday and the house would begin to smell of cornbread, fried chicken, and squash casserole. When Sunday afternoon finally came, we could not wait to sink our teeth into the chicken and all she had been preparing. All the time we were waiting to sit down to eat, she was creating a desire in us for that food well before it was available. She was premarketing her Sunday afternoon masterpiece on Friday and Saturday, and had no idea she was attracting paying customers to enjoy her food. (Well, even though we never paid for her cooking, I think we would have.)

The same is true when you market your book. Don't miss the opportunity to premarket your book and build a desire so people cannot wait for it to come out. Talk about your book, tell people what it is going to cover, and create your buying audience well in advance. Some pastors even preach on a portion from their book to give their congregation an idea of what it is going to offer.

A book is an extension of the author, and is no greater than the author.

Market your book to your tribe. Every writer has a tribe. These are the people who care about what you care about. They are your first market for your book. The keynote speaker I spoke of earlier said his tribe was his skydiving club, so he marketed his book to them, even before it was actually available.

Michael Hyatt wrote a book titled, *Platform*. His title creates a word picture. It says, "I am trying to speak to my people, but they cannot hear me, so I am going to build a platform that gets me high enough above the noise so I can reach them."

#7 – NOT USING THE BOOK COVER OR TABLE OF CONTENTS TO MARKET THE BOOK

The book's cover is the billboard for announcing your book to the world. The book's front cover should not have a picture of the author unless that author is famous. Rather, it should display the title and a representative image that will capture potential readers' attention and provoke curiosity. The back cover should not be a list of awards or academic degrees; it should explain to readers why they need to read the book.

The Table of Contents is the next most important part of the book. People will look at the cover, the back cover, maybe read the endorsements, but then they scan the Table of Contents. Whatever chapter title hits their felt need will entice them to actually turn to that chapter. Chapter titles that ask questions are a great tool to build curiosity in potential readers. Look at some of your favorite books and you will find great ideas on how to write an engaging Table of Contents.

#8 – NOT WRITING BOOKS 2, 3, AND 4

You get better with each book you write. What if John Maxwell and Mark Batterson never wrote more than one book? If you really feel called to write, then you should plan to write more than one book. If one of them takes off, trust me, people will be searching for your previous titles. Like every other endeavor—from sports to cooking—the more you do it, the better you get.

HOW TO COMMIT TO WRITING A BOOK

1. Make a commitment to spend a few minutes every day working on your book and stick to it. This

can range from research, to outlining, to writing. Mark this time on your calendar just like you would any other important appointment.

2. Consider assembling a writing team around you. There are people in your sphere of influence who would love to be part of your book writing project.

3. Determine the target audience, the main subject, and the questions you are going to answer.

4. Set specific, achievable deadlines, and celebrate when you achieve each one.

5. Talk to people within your sphere of influence and those who would benefit from your book. Sharing your message verbally can inspire commitment to getting that message down on paper. It will also jump start your premarketing efforts.

One woman came to me wanting to write a book about how God healed her as she cared for her husband who was suffering with Alzheimer's. As we set the date for publishing, I encouraged her to talk to her pastor and others who would help her market her book. She then told me she wanted the proceeds to go to hospice because of all the help they gave her in her husband's final days. I suggested she tell them of her idea in advance. The hospice invited her to speak and bring her book with her for a book signing. Every book sold and some people even gave her money to continue her ministry. She told me she didn't realize she had a ministry. Her book became her platform for her ministry.

Writing a book is like training for a marathon. Pay the entry fee and draw that line in the sand.

Ask Yourself...

- *What is my single-minded message for the book? What is the one key idea?*
- *Who is my "circle of influence," the people who can help me in the writing, reviewing, and marketing of my book?*
- *What commitment am I going to make to myself in writing this book? What is my plan of attack?*
- *What is my plan for editing?*
- *Have I thoughtfully considered the elements of my book, such as the cover, that will help its marketing?*

- CHAPTER 5 -

REASONS WHY TO PUBLISH

As I present the topic of writing books to individuals and large groups, I am always challenged with the final question, "Why should I publish my book?" I can sum it up in nine reasons. If you can identify with more than one of them, you should seriously consider publishing your manuscript.

1. **Someone you trust and value said you ought to write a book** sharing your experience and/or message. Nothing is as inspiring as someone telling you that your testimony is great, your message is great, and you should write a book.

2. **God called you to write a book.** Many of the great Christian writers of our day will tell you it came down to obeying the prompting or voice of God.

They say, "I feel like God asked me to do this." Very seldom do I hear, "I have no desire to do this, but God said to write a book." Desire and direction are many times mixed together.

3. **You want to make an impact.** You want to bring about change in the world and make a difference. When the passion to share your message is so strong you feel compelled to do something, then it might be time for you to write a book and unbottle the message within you.

4. **You have a desire to establish your teaching in print.** I am so thankful Charles Spurgeon published his sermons each week for people to enjoy. Because of that simple step, many, including myself, have enjoyed reading or studying from his teachings.

5. **Sales.** You have a message you believe people will buy, so you want to get it in book form. While money alone should never be the motivator to write and publish, many would be able to supplement their income if they wrote. I meet pastors all the time who are losing opportunities to not only influence others, but to also add to their income stream.

6. **You want to expand your message to places beyond your location.** There is an audience outside your immediate circle and you know you can reach them with a book. Think beyond your neighborhood to the state, the nation, and even the world.

7. **You want to leave legacy for future generations.** This could simply be people within your family or it could be your tribe of like-minded thinkers across the future. You want your testimony, your message, and what you have learned to be recorded. You don't want to leave this earth without telling your story.

8. **Creative desire.** You love to write. It is your gift, so you write to fulfill it. You really enjoy writing and it makes you happy.

9. **It is your business card.** You are good at what you do and want to use your book to introduce yourself when speaking and ministering. There is no better "leave behind."

Ask Yourself...

- *What are the reasons motivating me to publish?*
- *Do I need an author coach, an editor, or both to help me write my book?*
- *What is the next step I need to take to see my dream come true?*

APPENDIX

HOW TO GET STARTED WRITING YOUR BOOK

STEP 1	BEFORE YOU BEGIN TO WRITE

It is exciting to write a book, but it can also be a daunting prospect. There are a lot of steps and stages you must progress through to go from having an idea for a book to holding a finished copy in your hand. This guide is meant to share some helpful information so you can see the "big picture" of how to get started writing your book.

A. Determine Where You Are in the Writing Process

The first step is to determine where you are in the writing process. Every book has a starting point and progresses through a natural series of stages before it lives in the real world. Which stage are you in at this moment?

- It's just an idea in my head; I don't have anything written.
- I have some writing on the topic of my book, either handwritten or typed notes.
- I have an organized outline and a title, but that's about it.
- I have different parts of the book written, but I haven't pulled them together yet.
- I have a rough draft completed.
- I have a manuscript I've revised several times. I am ready to move forward to editing.

Once you know where you are, you can determine how much farther you have to go, and you can start identifying the resources you might need.

B. Start Setting Goals

One thing you can do no matter what stage you are in is to begin setting goals for your writing. Having a series of goals and a time line for completing them will help you break your book project down into sequential steps and help you continue your forward progress.

The trick is to set well-defined goals that are a stretch, but reachable. The best goals are SMART goals:

S = Specific
M = Measurable
A = Achievable
R = Relevant
T = Timed for a specific completion date

When you reach one goal, set another!

C. Follow Basic Formatting Guidelines

Be certain you are following some basic formatting guidelines, especially if you plan to self-publish your book. This will allow you to set up your book file correctly from the start.

Do work on the computer. Publishing is digital nowadays. When you are ready to turn in a manuscript, you will do so by uploading your computer file through a website, attaching the file to an email, or mailing in a flash drive. Gone are the days when you mailed a hard printed copy to your publisher.

Do not try to format your document to the size you want your finished book to be. Designing the interior of the book comes later when you are with a publisher. They have specific publishing software to do this. Stick with the standard 8 ½ x 11 computer page with the standard margins.

HERE ARE SOME MORE GENERAL RULES TO FOLLOW:

- Microsoft Word is the most common word processing program to use. If you are going to use another software program, make sure its files are compatible with Microsoft Word.
- Make sure you know the basics of the word processing program you are going to use. You will want to know how to copy and paste sections to move them around as well as how to insert a page break. If you are using footnotes or endnotes, understand how your computer program can set them up for you.
- Type in 12-point font. Twelve-point font is the standard size type in printed books. If you are having trouble seeing the words in 12 point, change the "zoom" feature on your computer screen; do not increase the size of the font.
- Type in regular type, not in all bold, all italics, or all capital letters. All bold, all italics, and all capital

letters are distracting for the reader and considered unprofessional.

- Create one document or one file for your book. Do not type every chapter in a separate document or file. This is because your editor and publisher will need one complete file, and they may even charge you extra if they have to pull all the pieces together.
- Let the computer naturally wrap your text around to the next line. Do not hit the enter key when you get close to the right-hand margin as you would with a manual typewriter. If you do this, there will be problems when the book interior is designed.
- When you want the next section of writing to start on a fresh page, insert a hard page break. Do not hit the enter button repeatedly until the words on your screen move to the next page. Doing so will cause problems when the book interior is designed.

If you already know which company you are going to use as your book publisher, be sure to read their manuscript guidelines for how you are supposed to set up your manuscript for their specific process.

STEP 2   BEGIN TO WRITE

A. Determine Your Audience

There is a saying that if you are writing a book for everybody, you are writing a book for no one in particular. Great authors write with a reader or an audience in mind. Are you writing a book for single mothers? Are you writing a book for business leaders? Are you writing to reach a young adult audience? It is important to focus on your audience because it influences how you will write and with what voice or tone. A book written for elementary school children reads much differently than a book on the same topic meant for adults.

So, who are you writing your book for? Identify that one primary audience. Sure, many other types of people may read your book, but there is always one group who needs your book the most. Describe in the best detail possible what your main reader is like, and as far as you can, determine what is the best way to talk to or communicate with them.

B.   Get Started

In other words, begin writing today. The hardest thing that most authors have to overcome is procrastination. The cemeteries and mausoleums surrounding us today are, in a sense, filled with books and stories that were never told and never written. Open your computer, grab a notebook, but do something now to overcome any desire to procrastinate. Even if you feel that you do not know enough to get started, make the decision to learn as you go.

Begin by just writing the thoughts you have about the subject or story. One of the most important steps in writing a book is to stop talking about it and get started. Many times authors talk about writing and can even tell their whole story, but they don't have anything written down. They have never gotten beyond their dream, idea, or vision. Start writing now! Even if it is messy and unorganized, it is now out of your head. Discover the truth that great writers have to get something written before they can really write their greatest work.

In fact, every good writer is a great rewriter, even the famous ones. Great writers know they must get their thoughts and ideas recorded before they can really begin to organize and clarify them into what will eventually form a well-written manuscript. If you think of a story that you want to include in your book, write it down. You will come back later to rewrite it and/or build around it. The problem most people have in getting started is they are trying to write a complete manuscript in their heads before they put anything on paper. They are trying to make the first draft the final manuscript.

Think of the beginning of your writing process like molding and shaping a chunk of clay into what will eventually become a beautiful vase. You must first drop the clay onto the wheel before you begin to mold and shape it. This step is simply to begin the process and watch what happens as you step out and start writing. Have you ever heard that it is easier to turn a car that is moving forward? Once you start moving, you will find that one thought written down leads to other thoughts you wouldn't have had if you had never written down the first thought.

STEP 3 ORGANIZE AN OUTLINE

A. Write Down Your Title Ideas

Jot down every title and subtitle that comes to mind for your book. One of these may end up being the final title of your book and another might be the subtitle. Rarely is your first title the one you end up with, but it marks the starting line for your race to finishing your book. Keep in mind your title is one guidepost to judge whether the ideas, principles, story lines, and points you wish to include actually belong in the book you are writing.

B. Write the Premise

When you start your book, it is important first to write a premise statement that establishes the main idea of your book. This is true for fiction and nonfiction books. Another way to think about the premise is that it is the basic concept, main story line, foundational principle, personal story, or instruction topic of your book. For example, if you are writing a book about how to raise children, you need to determine what the book is going to cover and how it will clearly summarize or specifically detail the ideas, principles, truths, teachings, and other material you have gleaned from your experience or research. Ask yourself, "What am I seeking to clearly communicate to my reader?" If you, the author, don't know what you are trying to communicate, you will never be able to communicate it clearly to the reader.

The premise should be brief and to the point. Start with two or three sentences at first. Imagine this is your "elevator speech," meaning imagine you are in an elevator with another person who asks, "What is your book about?" and you have thirty seconds before he gets off at the next floor to tell him. Once you have your short premise, expand it into one to three paragraphs, making certain that the basic idea of the book is clearly constructed with the necessary supporting details.

Your premise serves as the plumb line for communicating everything in the book. Every chapter, every poem, and every part of your story must be tied to the central premise and direction for your book, whether you are writing an autobiography, a novel, or a piece of nonfiction. If you stay within your premise, your book will not stray off topic.

C. Invite Feedback from Others

Once you have a premise written with the supporting details clearly explained, let other people read it. See what questions they ask. Ask for specific feedback. Doing so will enable you to add to the premise any additional content needed to answer questions potential readers might have.

Be sure to have people who know you and people who don't know you as well read your premise. This is because family members and close friends are likely to tell you "good job" which isn't all that helpful when you are looking to make improvements. People who are not tied to you emotionally will have some distance that may lead to more directed comments.

Here are some questions to ask people after they have read what you have done. Being specific will help you get back useable feedback.

1. Based on what you read, how would you summarize the main idea of the book?
2. Can you tell others the purpose of the book in your own words?
3. Is the reason for my writing the book clear?
4. What benefits do you think you would receive from reading this book?
5. Who do you think would be interested in this book?
6. Can you see a market for the book?
7. Would you buy the book? Why or why not?
8. What topics am I missing that need to be included in this book?

Once you have some feedback, go back and fine-tune the premise as clearly and sharply as you can, listing all the benefits you want the reader to receive from reading your book.

D. Create a Chapter Outline

Now it is time to list all of the major topics, ideas, concepts, story elements, and principles you believe should be covered in your book. This list will eventually be refined into your chapters. Don't worry right now about the order of the chapters. You can put an order to your chapters later. Right now you simply want to get the main concepts written down. Spend some time doing this. Once you have made your initial list of topics and chapters, let it sit for a few days and come back to it after you have had time to think on the material. Then add to and subtract from your list.

Once you have a list of chapter titles and topics, go back and write a paragraph or two with your main idea for each chapter. Just as the book needs a premise, each chapter needs a premise.

- What are you going to communicate in this chapter?
- What do you want the reader to learn?
- What is the material you want to share with the reader?
- What benefit will the reader get from this chapter?

- What will the reader further understand once they have read this chapter?
- What will the reader be able to do as a result of reading this chapter?
- How will this chapter change the reader?

STEP 4 — TURN YOUR OUTLINE INTO A MANUSCRIPT

You've constructed a road map for your book, now it is time to get started on the writing journey. This step contains specific tips on how to bring everything together to complete your manuscript. Up until now, you've only had the framework for your book. Now it is time to piece it all together and expand on the main points of your outline.

Follow the "C's" of communication. Remember, you are trying to convey a series of ideas and you want to be as clear as possible. Focusing on the following points will help your reader connect with and internalize your message.

A. Clarity

You want to write as simply, clearly, and directly as possible. Put your chapters in order so your message or story flows smoothly and understandably. You are not trying to impress the reader with your academic or philosophical knowledge. Use language that is straightforward and descriptive. If you write with clarity and communicate with words anybody can understand, you will reach those you are writing for.

B. Consistency

As you are writing, do not go off on rabbit trails; stay focused on and consistent with the premise. Every chapter needs to line up with the premise of the book. That is your gold standard. If you deviate too far from the premise, you are writing another book. Do not introduce confusing ideas and concepts that might be great for the reader to know, but that don't fit with the purpose of the book. Be consistent.

C. Caring

You want to connect with your reader, showing that you care about them and understand what they are searching for. Your reader needs to know you are on their side and that you are seeking to share out of a caring mind-set if the reader feels you are trying to speak down to them, be critical of them, or in any way use or abuse them, they will not be interested in continuing with your book. Be caring and people will read what you are saying, even if it sometimes contradicts what they believe or how they are living. To gain perspective, have someone else check your writing for the tone you are using.

D. Concise

Watch out for redundancy. Often a writer will say the same thing a dozen different ways. While repetition works well when communicating verbally, it doesn't communicate well in print. Be careful not to repeat the same phrases or stories over and over again throughout your book. Practice brevity, completing your thought with just the right nouns, diverse action verbs, and very descriptive adjectives and adverbs. This will season your writing just right.

E. Continuous

Keep your plot, message, and story moving. Don't bog down in a sideline so that your book loses momentum. It is a known fact that most readers never finish the books they purchase. Granted, some readers are lazy or find themselves distracted, but write so the book moves the reader through a continuous journey. Don't get waylaid in circular arguments or reasoning. Move forward. Start, focus, and continue through your vision to stay on course and finish strong. Picture a road map of where you want the reader to begin and where you want them to end. The chapters between the Introduction and Conclusion are the places they will need to visit to reach the end point.

STEP 5	FOLLOW THESE WRITING TIPS

A. Decide the "Person" or "Voice" You Are Writing In

What does this mean? Ask yourself if you are going to write your book in the first person singular or plural (I or we), second person (you), or third person (they). Be careful when you write to keep the "person" the same in each paragraph or section of your book. For example, if you are addressing the reader as "you" do not switch the person in the middle of the paragraph and start writing "we." Be consistent.

- You may prefer to be more removed and less direct when you write, so use the third person "they" as opposed to the more personal "we." Using "they" and "one" makes the style more neutral, distant, and abstract. For example:
  "One may think that all writers are experts in their subject."
- If you are going to include yourself with the readers, then use "we." For example: "We think that all writers are experts in their subject."

- You may also choose to simply address the reader directly. For example: "You may think all writers are experts in their subject."

Be consistent in the person you choose within each paragraph. Also, avoid preaching at the reader. When you do use the word "you," be certain that it is more of a teaching or personal style and less of an accusatory style. If you come across as being judgmental or condemning, the reader may not want to read what you are writing and your message will be lost.

B. Use Proper Sentence Structure

Do not write in sentence fragments; write in complete sentences. Proper sentence structure includes a subject and a predicate. A sentence fragment leaves the reader hanging with an unfinished thought.

Also, avoid the use of excessively long sentences. Some authors like to write with sentences that are paragraph length. Compound and complex sentences are needed when writing, but avoid excessive usage since they bog a reader down and often obscure your train of thought. Clear communication requires clarity. Keep your sentences crisp and to the point so the flow of your thought keeps consistently moving forward.

C. Use Verbs, Nouns, and Pronouns Properly

Strong writing uses lots of action verbs, specific nouns, and highly descriptive adjectives and adverbs. Just avoid repetition, however.

Change your adjectives and adverbs to add variety and interest to your writing. Also, watch out for "filler words" like very, so, just, and really. Although we often speak this way, "filler words" add little value to your writing.

For the strongest read, use an active voice instead of a passive voice. In a sentence written in an active voice, the subject of the sentence performs the action. In a sentence written in a passive voice, the subject receives the action. Examine the two sentences below and ask yourself which one sounds better and moves the action along.

- Active: The dog bit the man.
- Passive: The man was bitten by the dog.

Also, use the active form of the verb when you are writing in past tense rather than the passive forms for the same reason.

- Active: The man went to the store frequently.
- Passive: The man was going to the store frequently.

77

D. Do Not Be Excessive

Many first-time writers make the mistake of over emphasizing their points. They want to make sure the reader doesn't miss the importance of what they are saying, so they add extra punctuation or format the text in bold, italics, or all capital letters.

Putting multiple question marks or exclamation marks at the end of your sentences to "drive a point home" is actually counterproductive. It can turn the reader off for two possible reasons: 1) they might feel insulted that you think they are not smart enough to understand what you are saying, or 2) they may begin to doubt your authority since you continually rely on multiple question marks or exclamation marks for emphasis rather than make your point with direct writing. Keep in mind, it is very wearisome for the reader to wade through lots of unnecessary punctuation.

Another thing to avoid is excessive use of bold type, italics, or all capital letters. While this formatting, when used properly, can help a reader understand your organization of the book or the unique points of your message, over use of any of this formatting is unprofessional and makes the book visually confusing.

Bold type is best used for chapter titles, headings within your chapters, or a single word in a sentence that needs emphasis or definition. Italics is best used for calling attention to a single word in a sentence that needs emphasis or for when you need to call attention to a scripture verse or quote. Writing words all in capital letters should be used very sparingly. This is because using all caps comes across in print as if you are yelling at the reader.

E. Give Proper Attribution

Using material from another source can be a great way to enrich your book, support your writing, and educate the reader. However, you must give proper attribution when you quote from or paraphrase passages from books, magazines, the internet, or other sources. Remember, plagiarism is a crime, which means when you take or refer to specific ideas from other sources you must be certain that you give credit to the source with the proper citation, such as a footnote, endnote, or bibliography.

However, if the idea or expression is a common cliché, aphorism, or historical quote that is so general it has become part of the conventional wisdom, no quotation or citation is needed. For example, if you use a phrase like "A penny saved is a penny earned," it is not necessary to cite Benjamin Franklin as the author of this common aphorism.

With quotes from other historical figures, like George Washington or Winston Churchill, you may cite their works, but it is not always necessary to identify the exact reference work and page number from which the original quote was taken from. You might quote the historical figure and identify the source from the internet, which has many websites of famous quotes. If you do, simply reference the site in your chapter notes or endnotes.

When citing any printed reference, be certain to provide the author, the work, the publishing city and company, the date of publication, and the page number the quote was taken from. We will not go into the format and placement of citations, but the resource you want to use for more information and proper instruction is *The Chicago Manual of Style*. This style guide is the editing "bible" for correct grammar, punctuation, formatting, and more for published books.

STEP 6 HAVE YOUR MANUSCRIPT EDITED

Editing is essential to having a professional, trade-quality book. Consider it an investment in your writing. Editing will make your book more attractive to traditional publishers, self-publishers, literary agents, and the public.

It is impossible to edit your own writing to the highest level of excellence, even when you follow all the above tips and review your manuscript several times. Very few authors have been trained as editors, and even best-selling authors look to editors to correct and polish their writing. Simply stated, you are too close to the work to see what can be done to improve its strengths and correct its weaknesses.

There are three broad categories of editing that most authors choose from. Two of these categories, the Developmental level and the Line level, help an author improve the quality and content of his or her writing. The other category, the Basic level, helps an author catch all the technical mistakes of grammar, punctuation, verb agreement, and syntax.

A. Developmental Editing

This is the most comprehensive type of editing and touches the book on all levels. A Developmental Edit is at least two rounds of editing and typically includes the Line Edit and Basic Edit levels. It is designed to fix the "big picture" structure of the manuscript to increase the book's marketability. It is for those who have a solid idea, but are not sure how to organize and present the material.

Choose a Developmental Edit if any of the following holds true for you:

- Your book does not have chapters or paragraphs.
- You do not know the order in which to tell your story or present your message.
- You need to know exactly where to add more detail to expand your book.
- Your book is too long and you do not know what to delete or shorten.
- You want specific guidance on how to rewrite your manuscript.

B. Line Editing

Eighty percent of books need a Line Edit. A Line Edit typically includes a Basic Edit. Line Editing focuses on improving the flow and readability of your work so your message or story is clearly understood by the reader. Hard to understand sentences are rewritten, incomplete thoughts are finished, passive to active voice changes are made, paragraph and sentence length are adjusted, and transitions between thoughts and chapters are strengthened. Simply stated, Line Editing helps improve the clarity and completeness of the content.

Choose a Line Edit if any of the following holds true for you:

- You have wordy or awkward sentences.
- You have long paragraphs or long sentences.
- Your writing is choppy and does not flow smoothly.
- You do not have strong transitions between thoughts, paragraphs, and chapters.
- You have been unsure of your word choice throughout the book.

C. Basic Editing

A Basic Edit is also known as a copy edit or technical edit. This type of editing is what most people think about as proofreading (even though proofreading is a term that applies to a later process in the physical creation of a book). All books should receive a Basic Edit because another set of eyes is beneficial in catching the errors the author has missed because he or she can't see them anymore. For example, traditionally published books go through two to three rounds of Basic Editing.

A Basic Edit should be conducted to the standards of *The Chicago Manual of Style*, which is the style guide that published books should follow. A Basic Edit checks over the "rules" of writing, such things as spelling, grammar, punctuation, verb-tense agreement, subject-predicate agreement, formatting of block quotes, and checking the bibliography for missing information and correct formatting.

Choose a Basic Edit if any of the following holds true for you:

- You cannot remember the proper usage of commas, semicolons, ellipses, and other punctuation marks.
- You switch from 1st person to 3rd person and are not sure which voice to use.
- You are confused about the correct verb tense to use.
- You want another set of eyes to correct typos, spelling errors, missing words, and incomplete sentences.
- You want to make sure your writing is technically correct according to *The Chicago Manual of Style*.

D. Still Not Sure?

We strongly recommend that you have an editorial diagnostic done on your manuscript to describe what you can do and what a professional edit can do to take your manuscript to the next level. Clearly identify what you are looking for in an edit, and then talk to several editors for their opinions and their prices.

Remember as said previously, awkward writing and errors in your manuscript will:

- Diminish or limit the sales of your book.
- Embarrass you and detract from your credibility as a writer.
- Often cause the reader to stop reading the book.
- Limit positive reviews online and word-of-mouth recommendations.
- Keep bookstore agents from choosing your book for their shelves.

Authors may try to save some money by initially skipping editing. This can be a costly mistake that can have a negative impact in the long run. Investing in the quality of your manuscript through professional editing will enhance sales, take your writing to the highest publishing level, and make reading your book an easy and enjoyable experience for your readers.

Now, it's time to get started, push through, and finish your book with excellence!

WORKS CITED

Batterson, Mark. *Draw the Circle: The 40 Day Prayer Challenge*. Grand Rapids: Zondervan, 2012.

Batterson, Mark. "You Have a Book in You," last modified April 17, 2013, http://www.markbatterson. com/uncategorized/you-have-a-book-in-you/#sthash.7dae0SEC.dpuf

Elliot, Elizabeth. *Through Gates of Splendor*. Carol Stream: Tyndale Momentum; 1981

Evans, Richard Paul. *The Christmas Box*. New York: Simon & Schuster, 1993. http://www.richardpaulevans.com/index.php/books/the-christmas-box

Hyatt, Michael. *Platform: Get Noticed in a Noisy World*. Nashville: Thomas Nelson, 2012.

Lawson James Gilchrist. *Deeper Experiences of Famous Christians*. Anderson: Warner Press, 2007.

Lord, Peter. *Hearing God*. Ada: Baker Books, 1988.

Ortberg, John. *Soul Keeping: Caring For the Most Important Part of You*. Grand Rapids: Zondervan, 2014.

Pope, Charles Wesley. *Is Life Worth Living*. Self Published Curley Printing Company, 1959.

Waltrip, Michael. *In the Blink of an Eye: Dale, Daytona and the Day that Changed Everything*. New York: Hyperion, 2011.

Warren, Rick. *The Purpose Driven Life*. Grand Rapids: Zondervan, 2002

Young, William Paul. *The Shack: Where Tragedy Confronts Eternity*. New York: Windblown Media, 2007. http://rare.us/story/rare-interview-with-wm-paul-young-author-of-the-the-shack/

THANKS AND ACKNOWLEDGMENTS

No book is really ever the work of just one man alone. There is always someone else involved who brings influence upon the author or the author's work. Sometimes the influence comes early, serving as a catalyst that births something within the author's soul. Other times, it comes later to help the author in the creative or writing process. No matter when the influence comes, it is a part of the final product, the published book.

I know this statement is true for me and for this book, for there are several people who had a part in helping me discover and finish the book you are holding.

I would like to thank Mark Batterson who not only inspired me to write myself but also taught me the real value of a published book. His thoughts on how a book can actually be an answer to someone's prayer inspired me to help as many people as possible to pursue their dreams to write.

I want to thank and acknowledge Dr. Larry Keefauver who also inspired me to write and helped me develop the desire and pattern to help many others do the same.

This book came from years of his influence and inspiration. He also helped me to write it.

Finally, I want to thank Michelle Johnston who has not only been a vital member of my team at Xulon Press, she has also been like a co-creator and editor for both of my first two books. She worked tirelessly on this book like it was her own and actually added the appendix at the end of the book to further help every ministry leader write and finish their own books.

CPSIA information can be obtained
at www.ICGtesting.com
Printed in the USA
FSHW012132210219

9 781545 630976